GRAPHIC BIOGRAPHIES

★ ★ ★ ★ ★ ★ ★ ★ ★

NATHAN HALE
REVOLUTIONARY SPY

by Nathan Olson
illustrated by Cynthia Martin
and Brent Schoonover

Consultant:

Wayne Bodle, PhD
Assistant Professor of History
Indiana University of Pennsylvania
Indiana, Pennsylvania

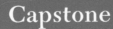

Capstone

Mankato, Minnesota

Graphic Library is published by Capstone Press,
1710 Roe Crest Drive, North Mankato, Minnesota 56003.
www.capstonepub.com

Library of Congress Cataloging-in-Publication Data
Olson, Nathan.
  Nathan Hale : revolutionary spy / by Nathan Olson; illustrated by Cynthia Martin and
Brent Schoonover
  p. cm.—(Graphic library. Graphic biographies)
  Summary: "In graphic novel format, tells the life story of Revolutionary War hero and spy
Nathan Hale"—Provided by publisher.
  Includes bibliographical references and index.
  ISBN: 978-0-7368-4968-5 (hardcover)
  ISBN: 978-0-7368-6199-1 (softcover pbk.)
  1. Hale, Nathan, 1755-1776—Juvenile literature. 2. United States—History—Revolution,
1775-1783—Secret service—Juvenile literature. 3. Spies—United State—Biography—Juvenile
literature. 4. Soldiers—United States—Biography—Juvenile literature. I. Title. II. Series.
E280.H2O45 2006
973.3'85'092—dc22   2005007894

Art and Editorial Direction
Jason Knudson and Blake A. Hoena

Designer
Ted Williams

Storyboard Artist
Barbara Schulz

Editor
Christopher Harbo

Editor's note: Direct quotations from primary sources are indicated by a yellow background.

Direct quotations appear on the following pages:
Pages 11, 15 (bottom), 25 (top), from *Documentary Life of Nathan Hale: Comprising all
    Available Official and Private Documents Bearing on the Life of the Patriot* by George
    Dudley Seymour (New Haven, Conn.: Private Publisher, 1941).
Pages 15 (top), 25 (bottom), from *Life of Captain Nathan Hale: The Martyr-Spy of the
American   Revolution* by I.
W. Stuart (Hartford, Conn.: F. A. Brown, 1856).

Printed in the United States   5798

★★★★★★★ TABLE OF CONTENTS

Chapter 1
Student and Teacher 4

Chapter 2
Soldier and Leader 10

Chapter 3
Daring Spy 16

Chapter 4
War Hero 22

More about Nathan Hale 28
Glossary 30
Internet Sites 30
Read More 31
Bibliography 31
Index 32

CHAPTER 1

STUDENT AND TEACHER

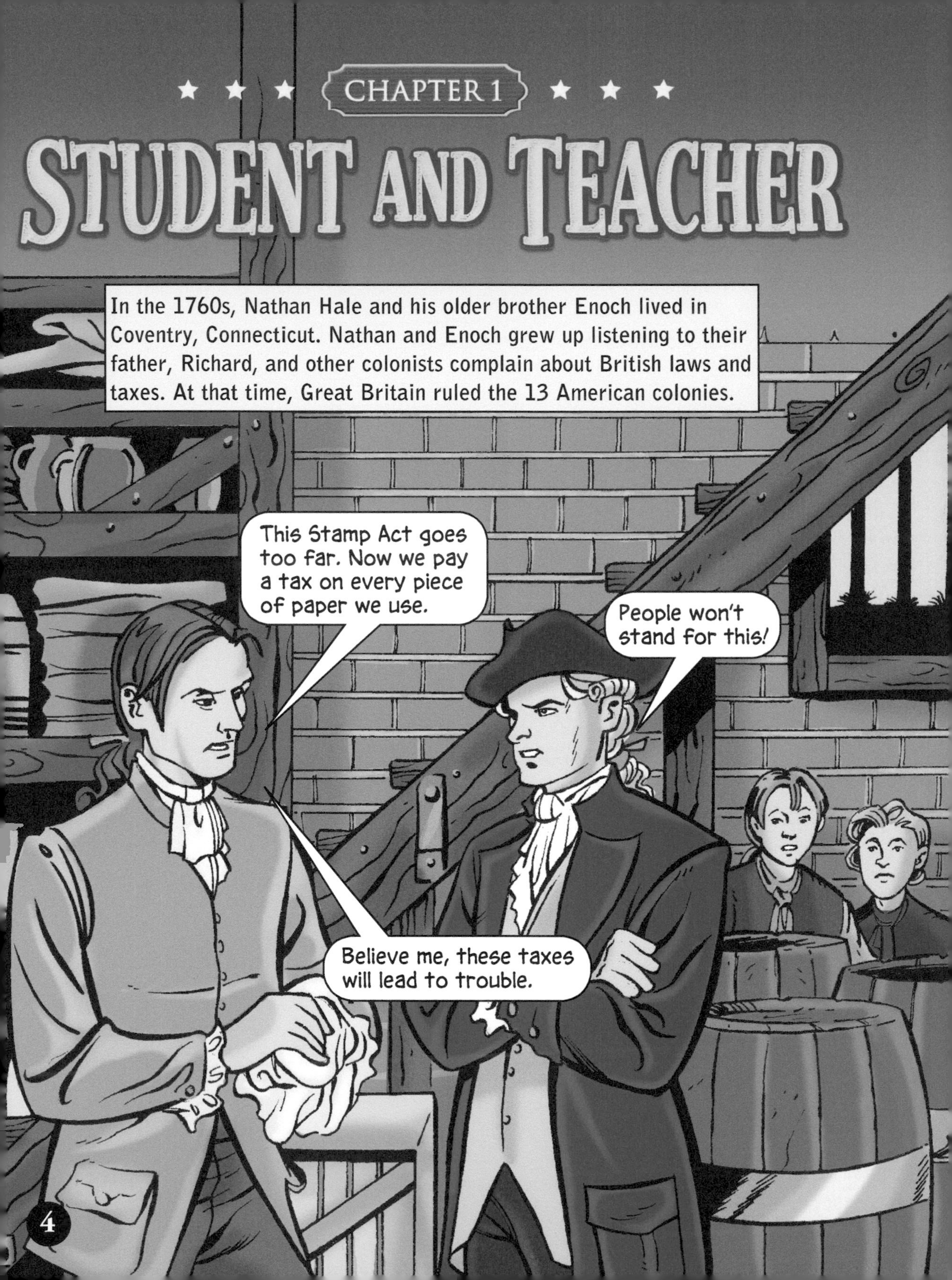
In the 1760s, Nathan Hale and his older brother Enoch lived in Coventry, Connecticut. Nathan and Enoch grew up listening to their father, Richard, and other colonists complain about British laws and taxes. At that time, Great Britain ruled the 13 American colonies.
This Stamp Act goes too far. Now we pay a tax on every piece of paper we use.
People won't stand for this!
Believe me, these taxes will lead to trouble.

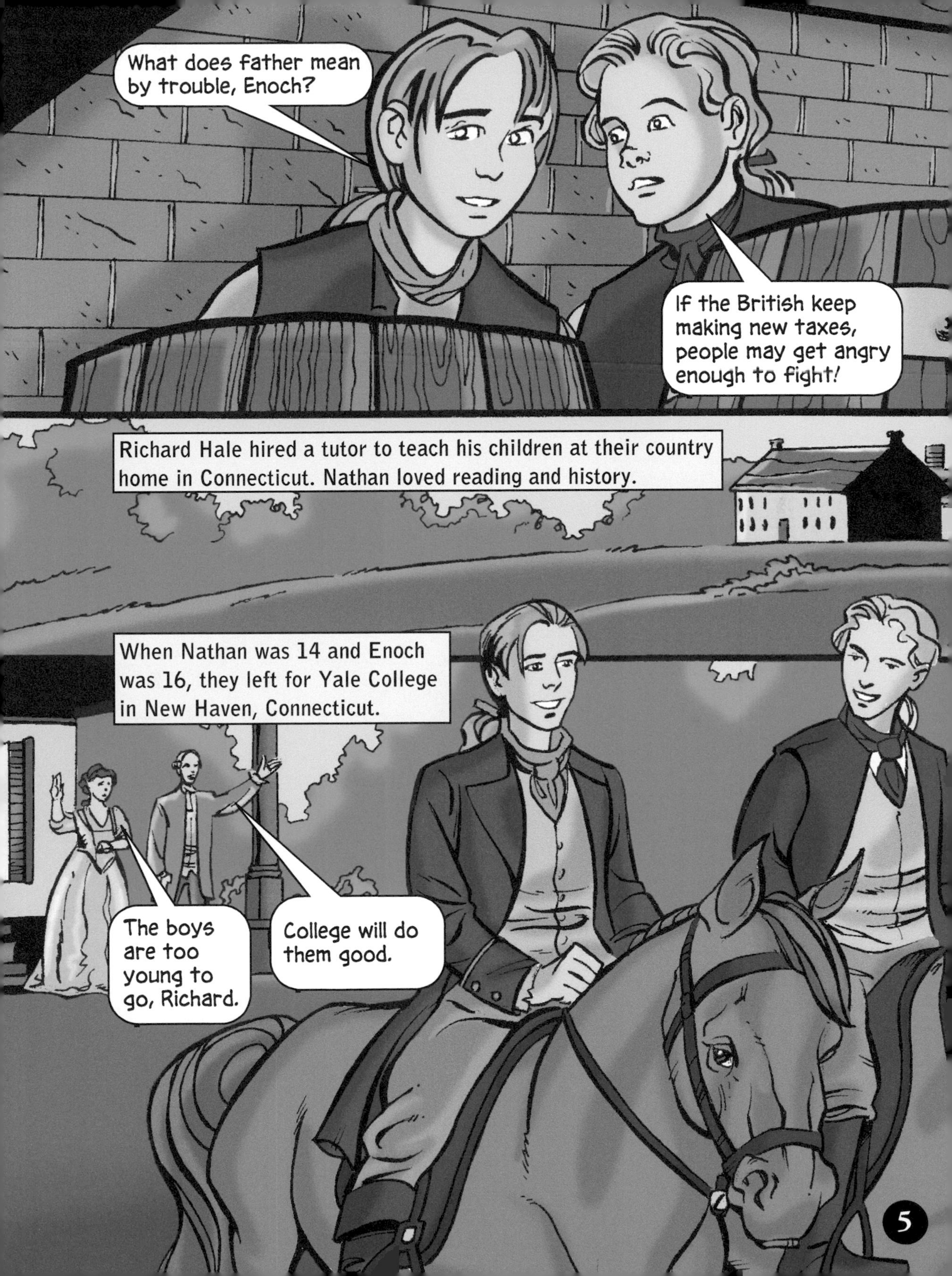
What does father mean by trouble, Enoch?
If the British keep making new taxes, people may get angry enough to fight!
Richard Hale hired a tutor to teach his children at their country home in Connecticut. Nathan loved reading and history.
When Nathan was 14 and Enoch was 16, they left for Yale College in New Haven, Connecticut.
The boys are too young to go, Richard.
College will do them good.

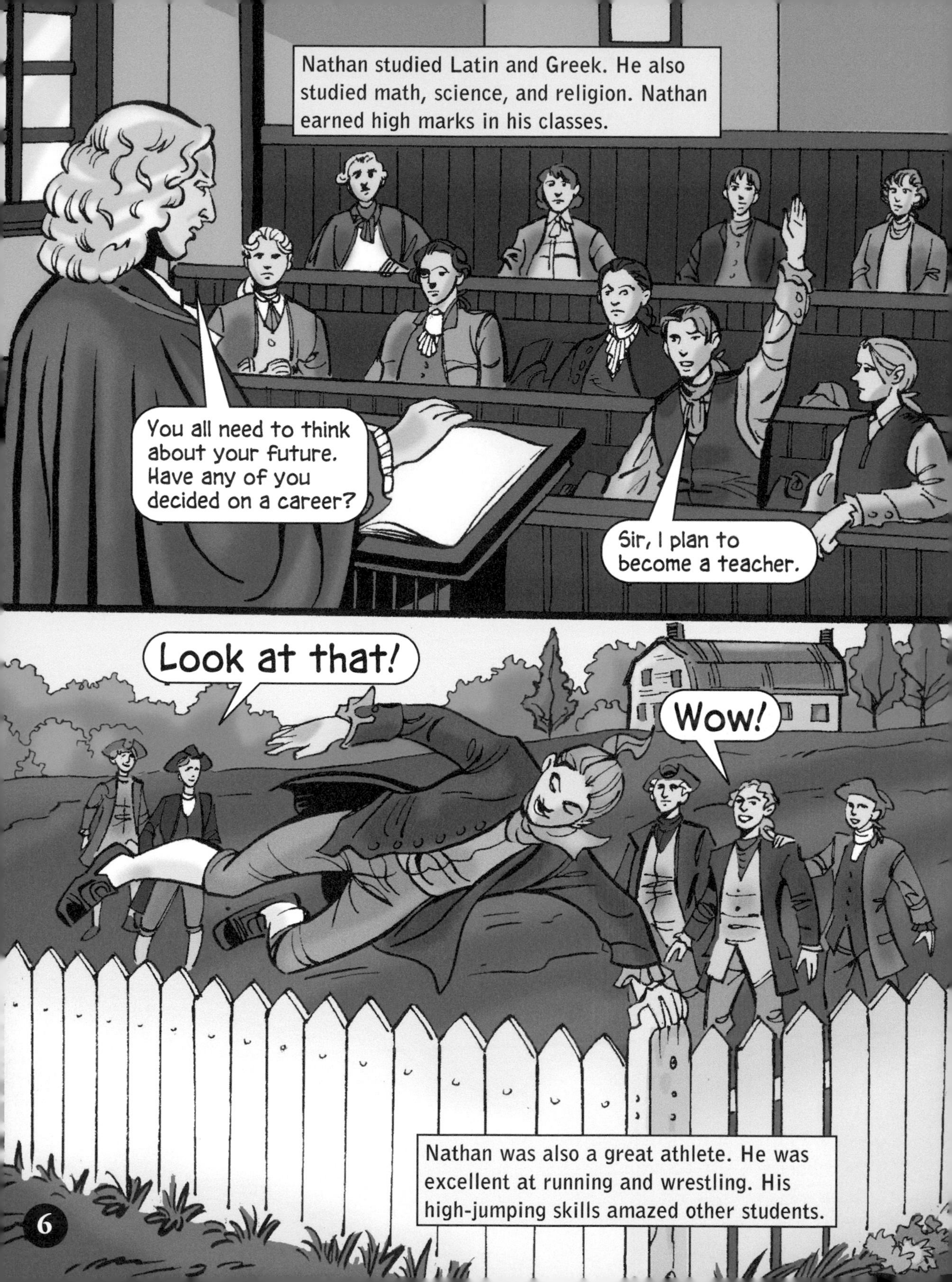
Nathan studied Latin and Greek. He also studied math, science, and religion. Nathan earned high marks in his classes.
You all need to think about your future. Have any of you decided on a career?
Sir, I plan to become a teacher.
Look at that!
Wow!
Nathan was also a great athlete. He was excellent at running and wrestling. His high-jumping skills amazed other students.

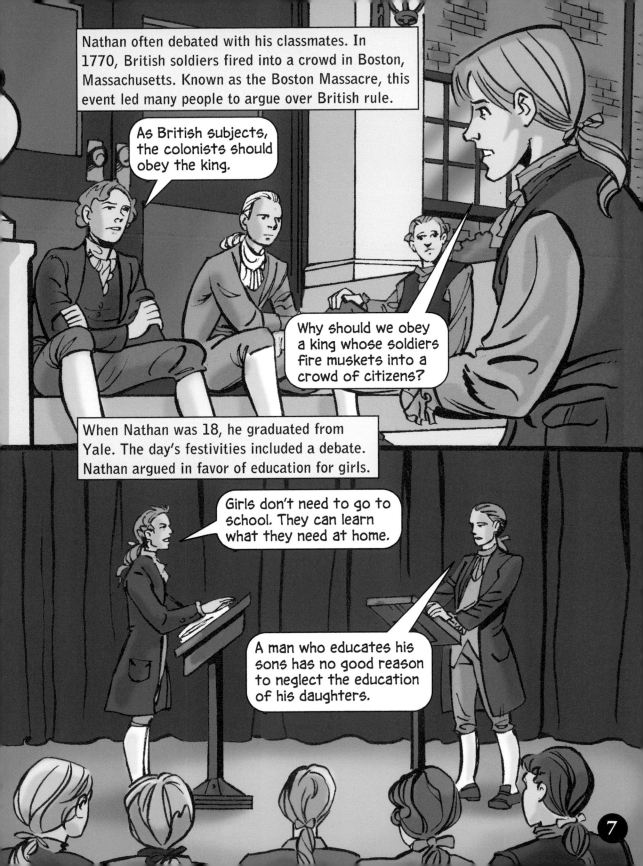

Nathan often debated with his classmates. In 1770, British soldiers fired into a crowd in Boston, Massachusetts. Known as the Boston Massacre, this event led many people to argue over British rule.

As British subjects, the colonists should obey the king.

Why should we obey a king whose soldiers fire muskets into a crowd of citizens?

When Nathan was 18, he graduated from Yale. The day's festivities included a debate. Nathan argued in favor of education for girls.

Girls don't need to go to school. They can learn what they need at home.

A man who educates his sons has no good reason to neglect the education of his daughters.

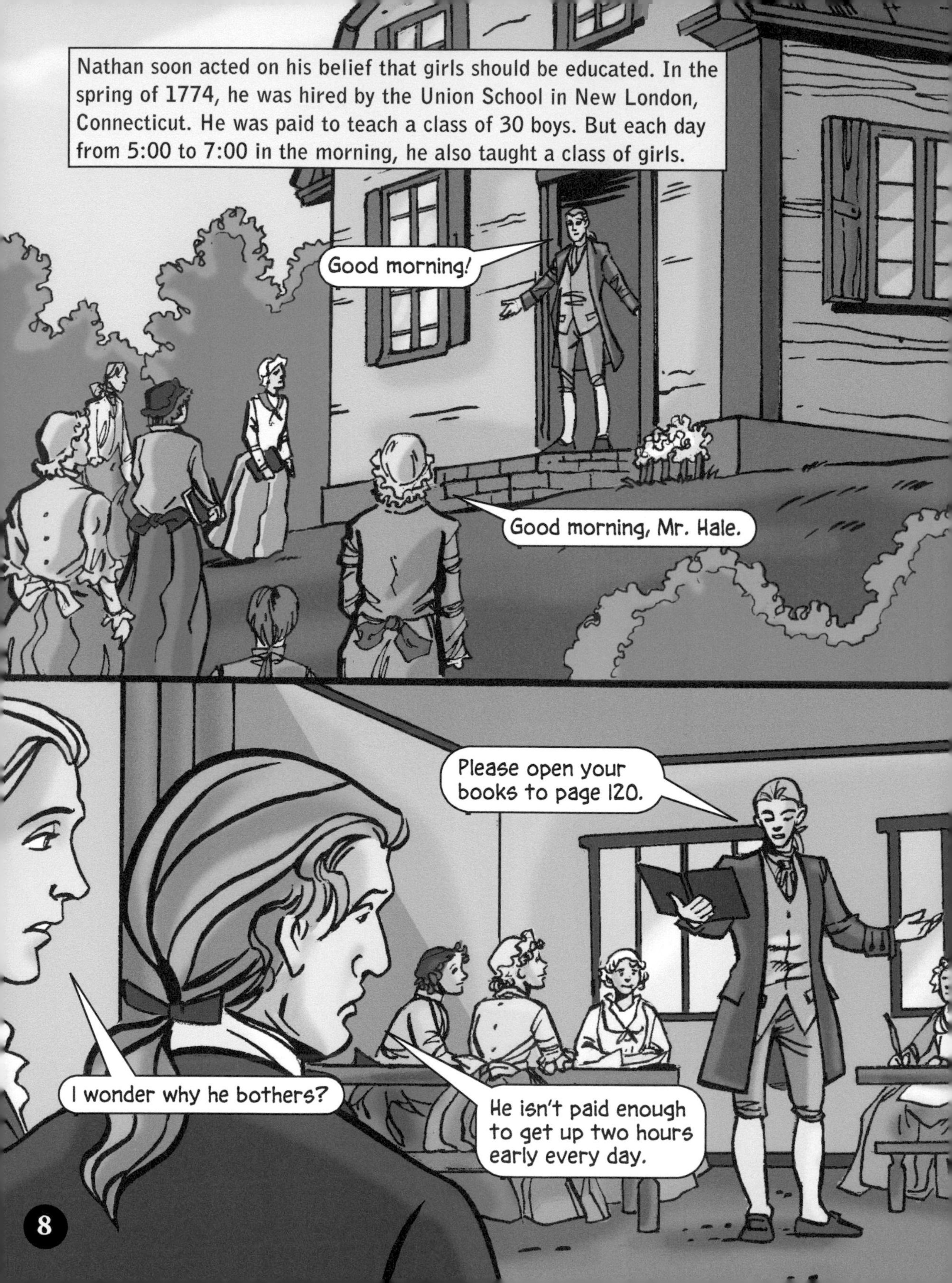
Nathan soon acted on his belief that girls should be educated. In the spring of 1774, he was hired by the Union School in New London, Connecticut. He was paid to teach a class of 30 boys. But each day from 5:00 to 7:00 in the morning, he also taught a class of girls.
Good morning!
Good morning, Mr. Hale.
Please open your books to page 120.
I wonder why he bothers?
He isn't paid enough to get up two hours early every day.

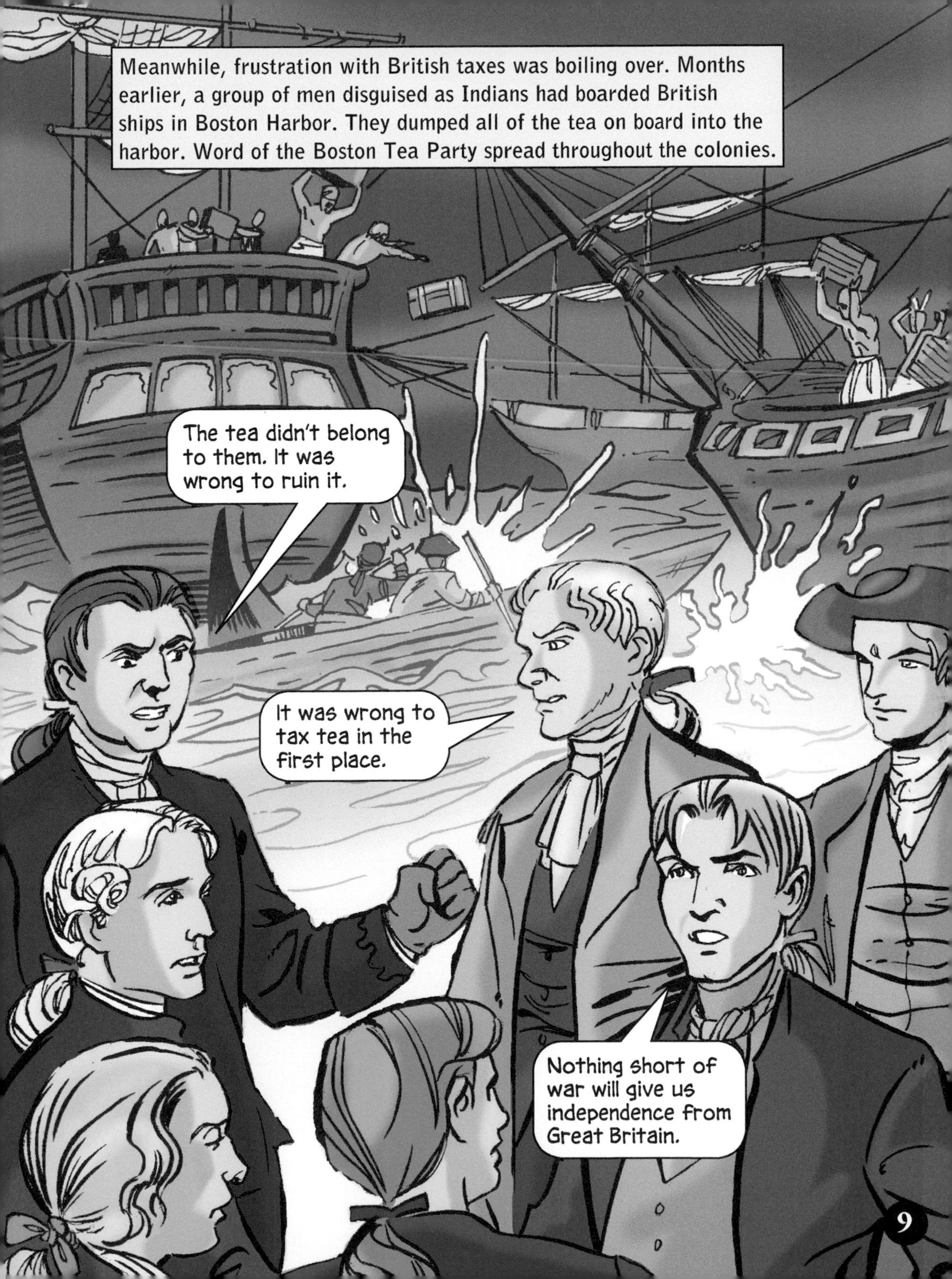
Meanwhile, frustration with British taxes was boiling over. Months earlier, a group of men disguised as Indians had boarded British ships in Boston Harbor. They dumped all of the tea on board into the harbor. Word of the Boston Tea Party spread throughout the colonies.
The tea didn't belong to them. It was wrong to ruin it.
It was wrong to tax tea in the first place.
Nothing short of war will give us independence from Great Britain.

CHAPTER 2

SOLDIER AND LEADER

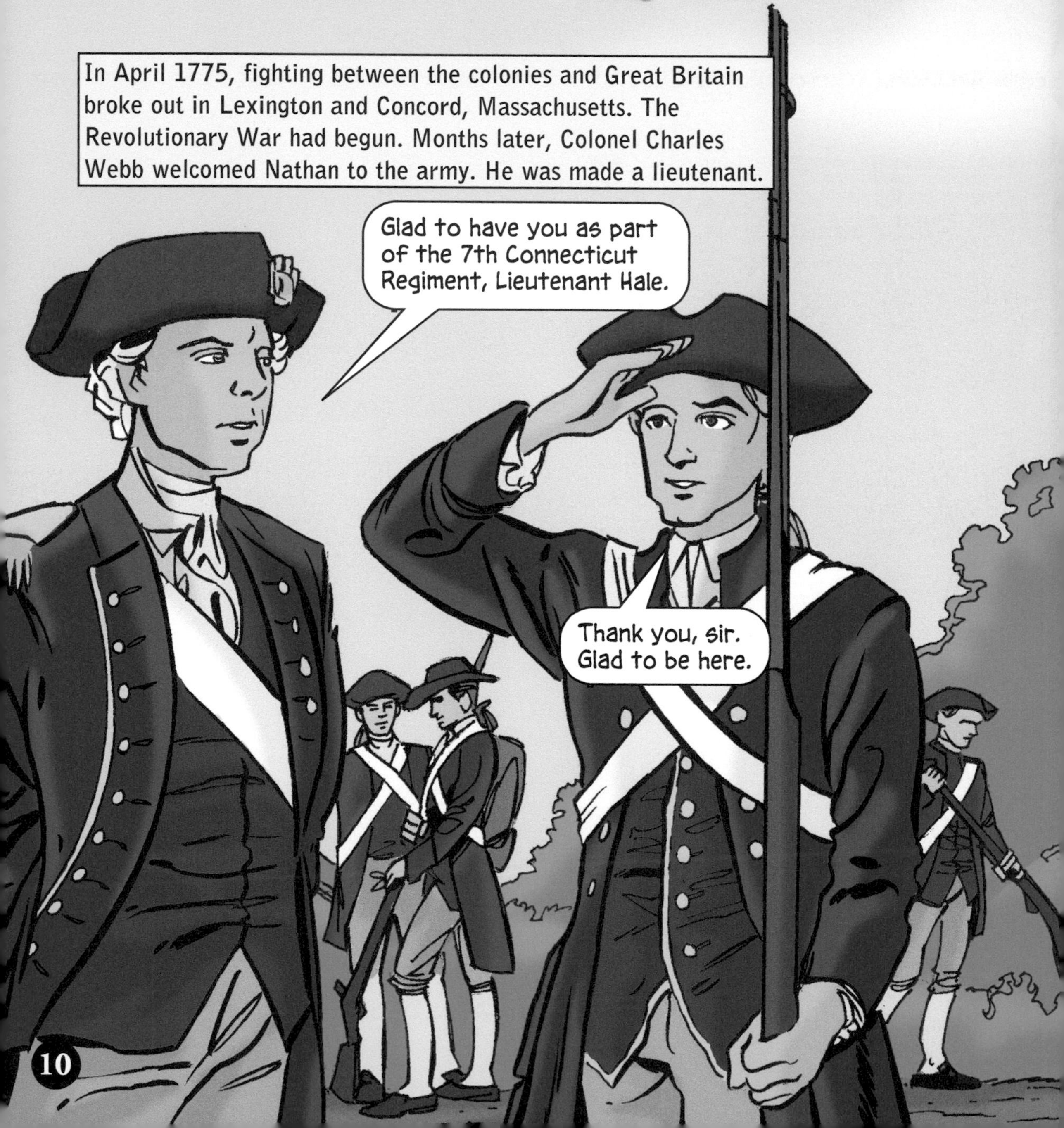
In April 1775, fighting between the colonies and Great Britain broke out in Lexington and Concord, Massachusetts. The Revolutionary War had begun. Months later, Colonel Charles Webb welcomed Nathan to the army. He was made a lieutenant.
Glad to have you as part of the 7th Connecticut Regiment, Lieutenant Hale.
Thank you, sir. Glad to be here.

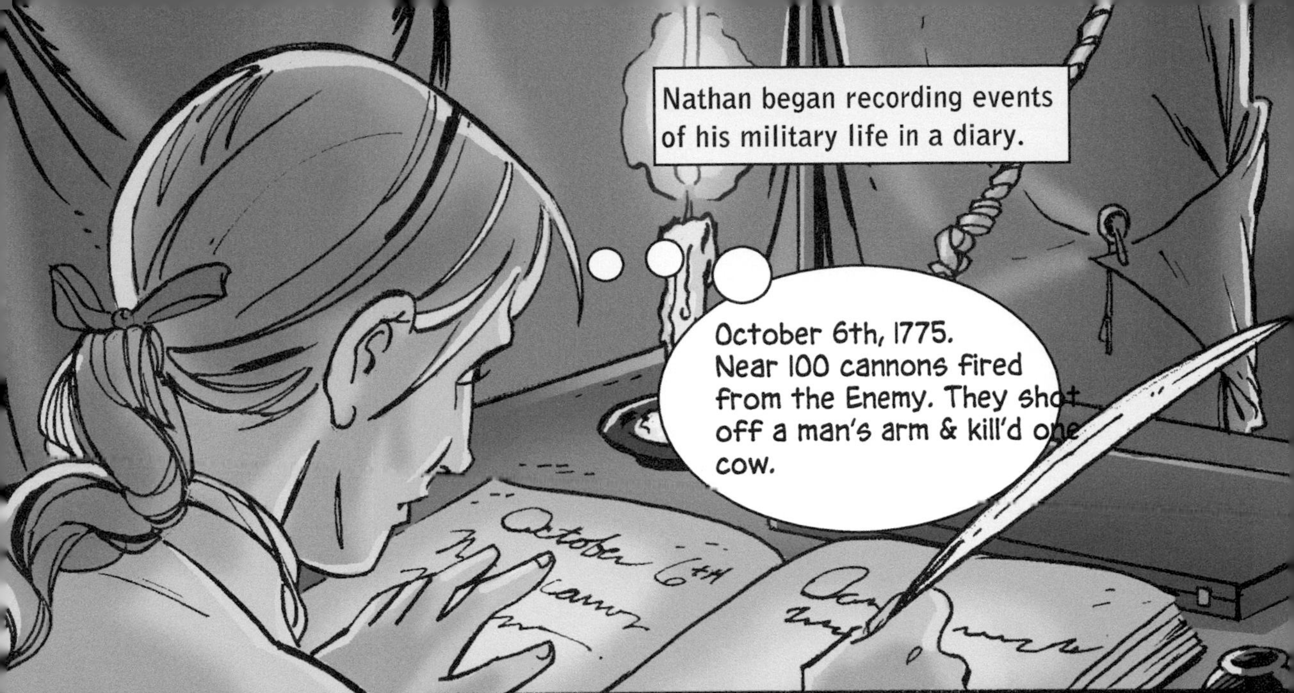
Nathan began recording events of his military life in a diary.
October 6th, 1775. Near 100 cannons fired from the Enemy. They shot off a man's arm & kill'd one cow.

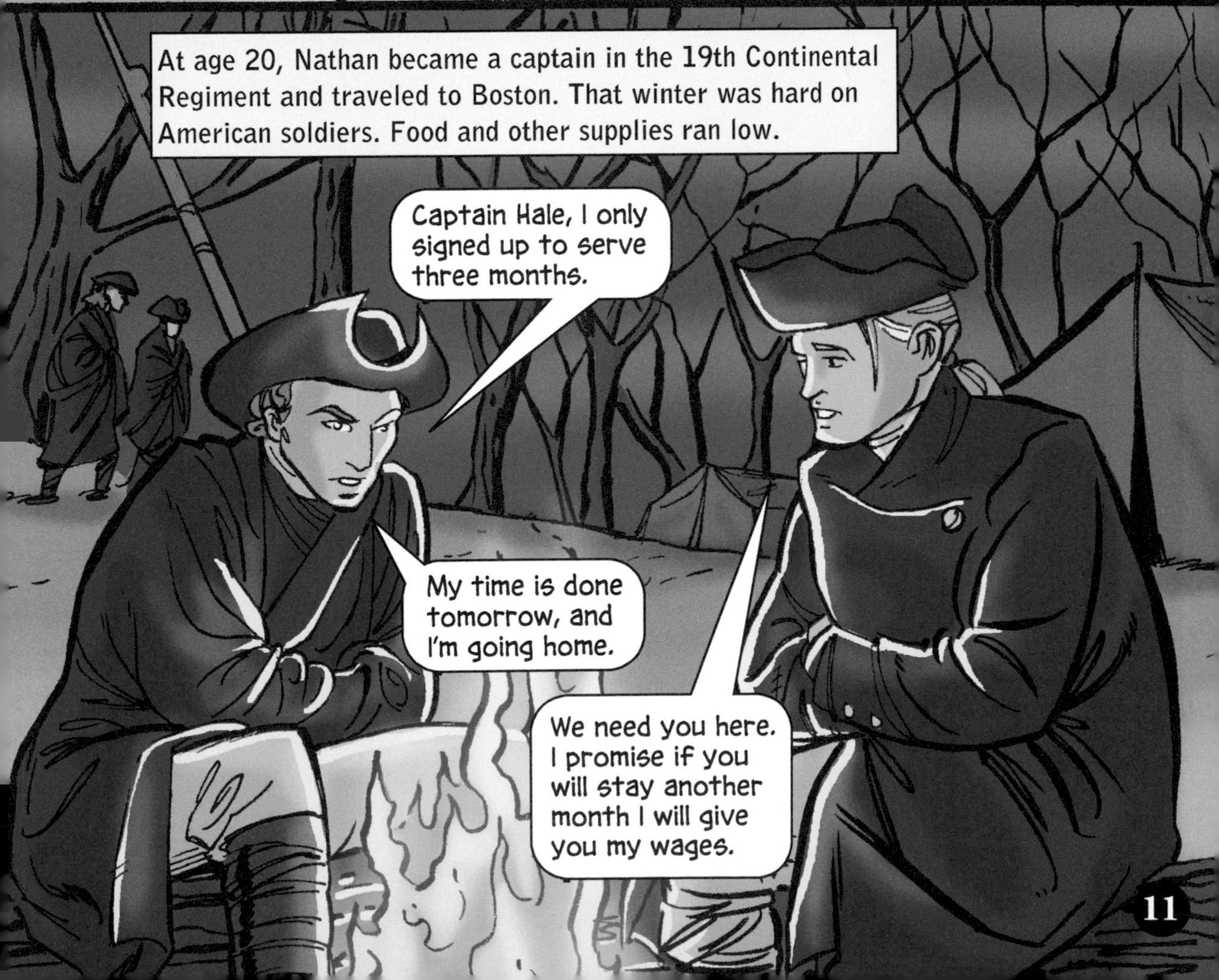
At age 20, Nathan became a captain in the 19th Continental Regiment and traveled to Boston. That winter was hard on American soldiers. Food and other supplies ran low.
Captain Hale, I only signed up to serve three months.
My time is done tomorrow, and I'm going home.
We need you here. I promise if you will stay another month I will give you my wages.

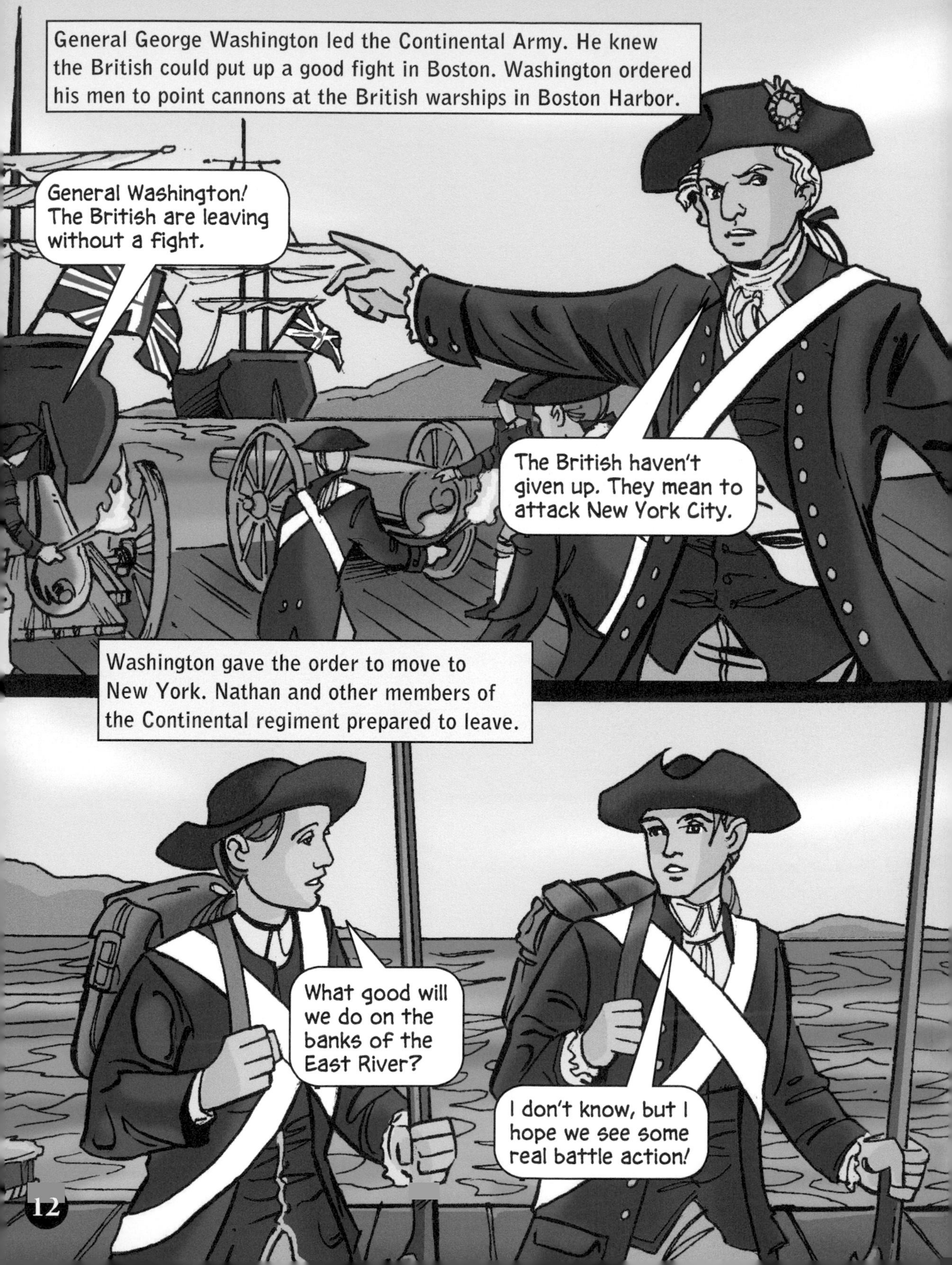
General George Washington led the Continental Army. He knew the British could put up a good fight in Boston. Washington ordered his men to point cannons at the British warships in Boston Harbor.
General Washington! The British are leaving without a fight.
The British haven't given up. They mean to attack New York City.
Washington gave the order to move to New York. Nathan and other members of the Continental regiment prepared to leave.
What good will we do on the banks of the East River?
I don't know, but I hope we see some real battle action!

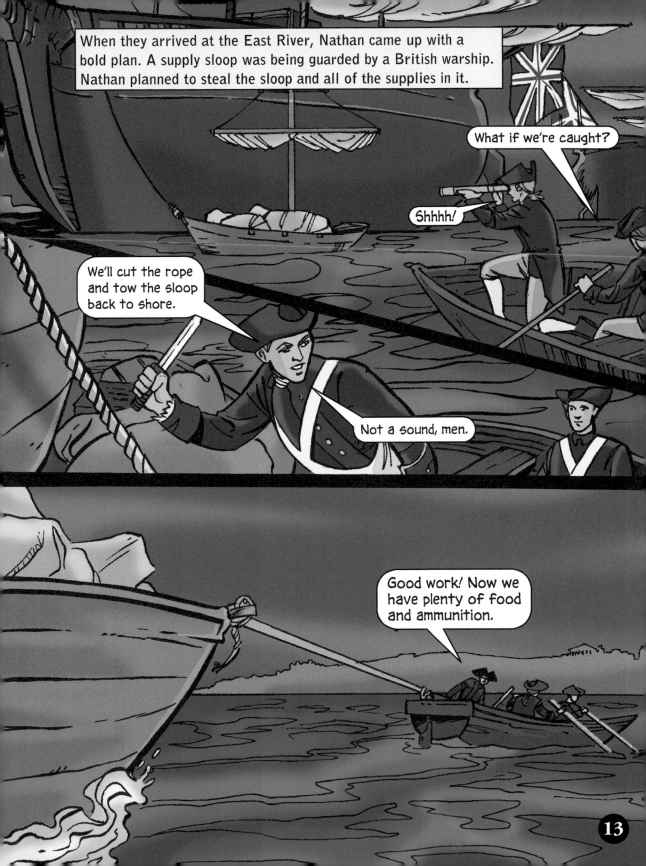

When they arrived at the East River, Nathan came up with a bold plan. A supply sloop was being guarded by a British warship. Nathan planned to steal the sloop and all of the supplies in it.

What if we're caught?

Shhhh!

We'll cut the rope and tow the sloop back to shore.

Not a sound, men.

Good work! Now we have plenty of food and ammunition.

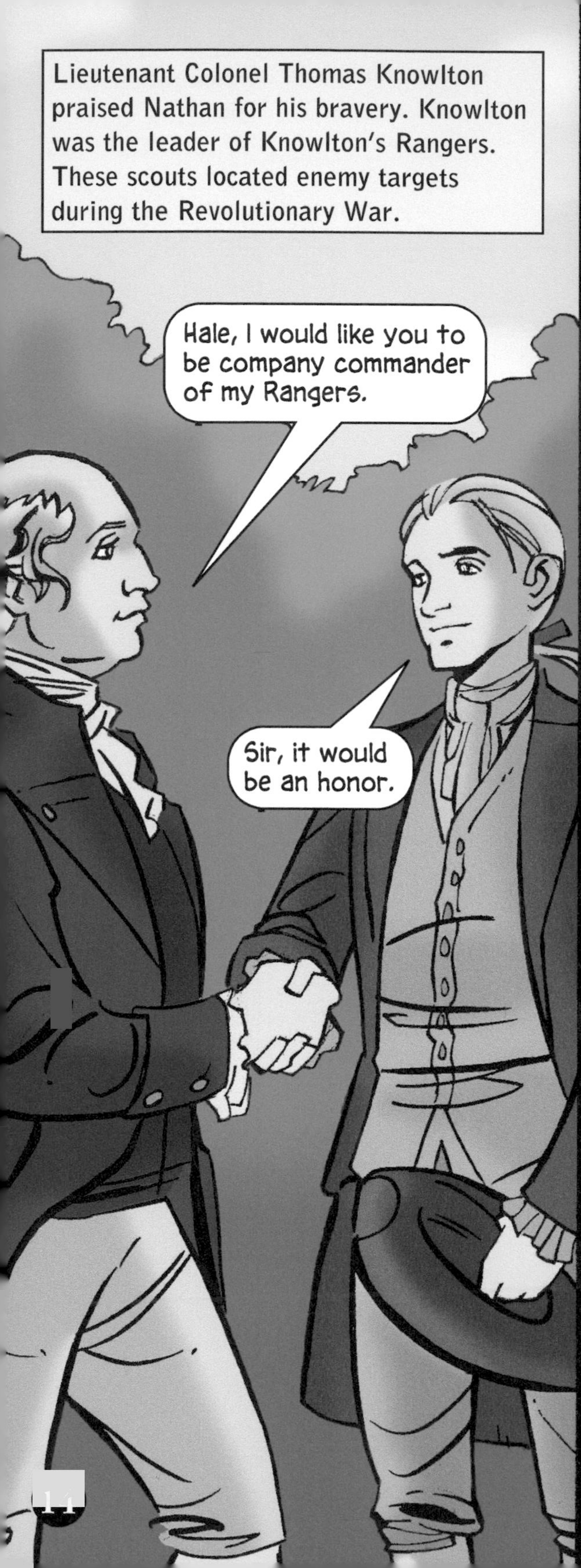
Lieutenant Colonel Thomas Knowlton praised Nathan for his bravery. Knowlton was the leader of Knowlton's Rangers. These scouts located enemy targets during the Revolutionary War.
Hale, I would like you to be company commander of my Rangers.
Sir, it would be an honor.

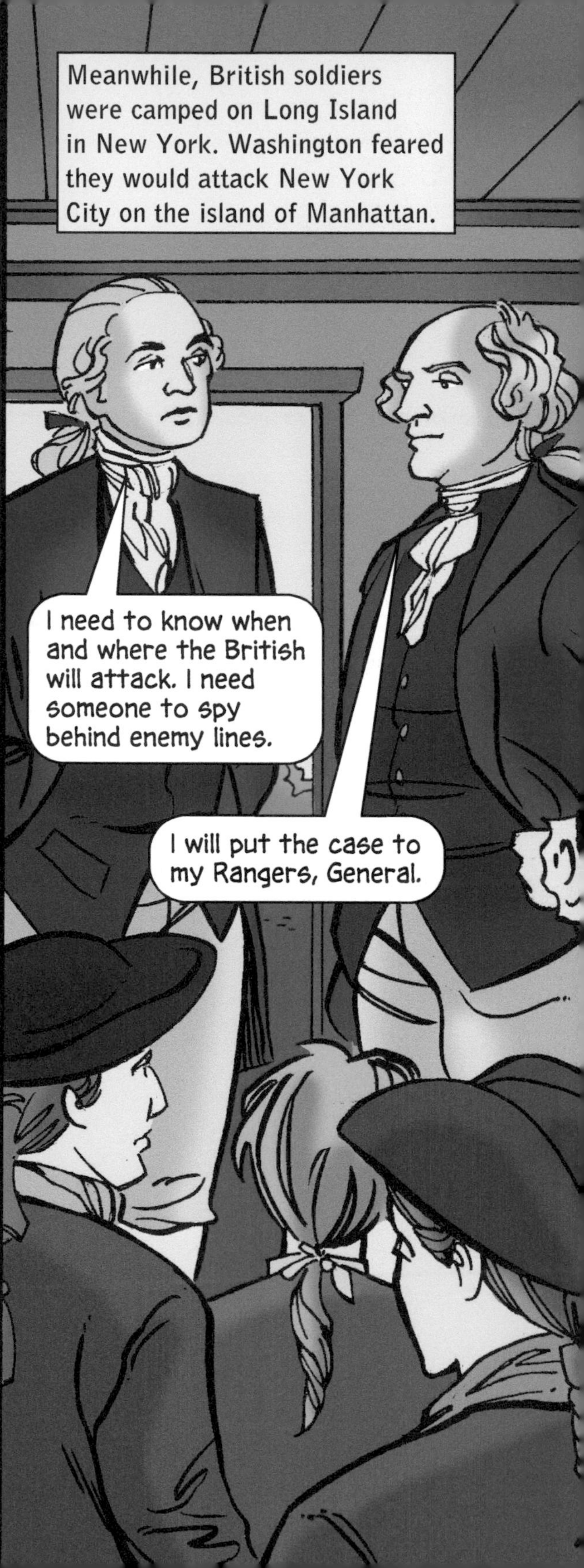
Meanwhile, British soldiers were camped on Long Island in New York. Washington feared they would attack New York City on the island of Manhattan.
I need to know when and where the British will attack. I need someone to spy behind enemy lines.
I will put the case to my Rangers, General.

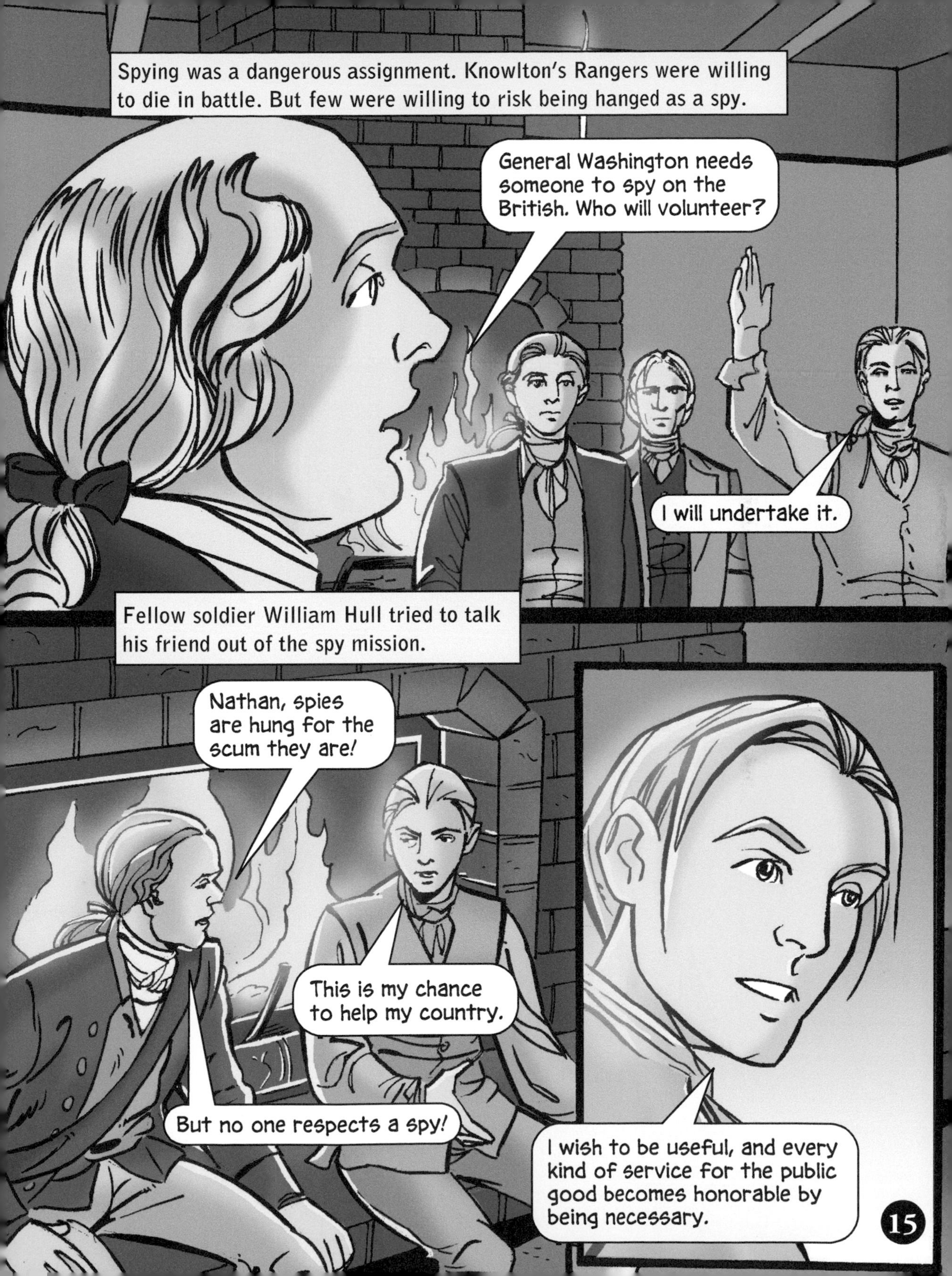
Spying was a dangerous assignment. Knowlton's Rangers were willing to die in battle. But few were willing to risk being hanged as a spy.
General Washington needs someone to spy on the British. Who will volunteer?
I will undertake it.
Fellow soldier William Hull tried to talk his friend out of the spy mission.
Nathan, spies are hung for the scum they are!
This is my chance to help my country.
But no one respects a spy!
I wish to be useful, and every kind of service for the public good becomes honorable by being necessary.

CHAPTER 3

DARING SPY

Disguised as a Dutch schoolmaster, Nathan headed for Long Island on September 12, 1776. He was eager to perform his mission.

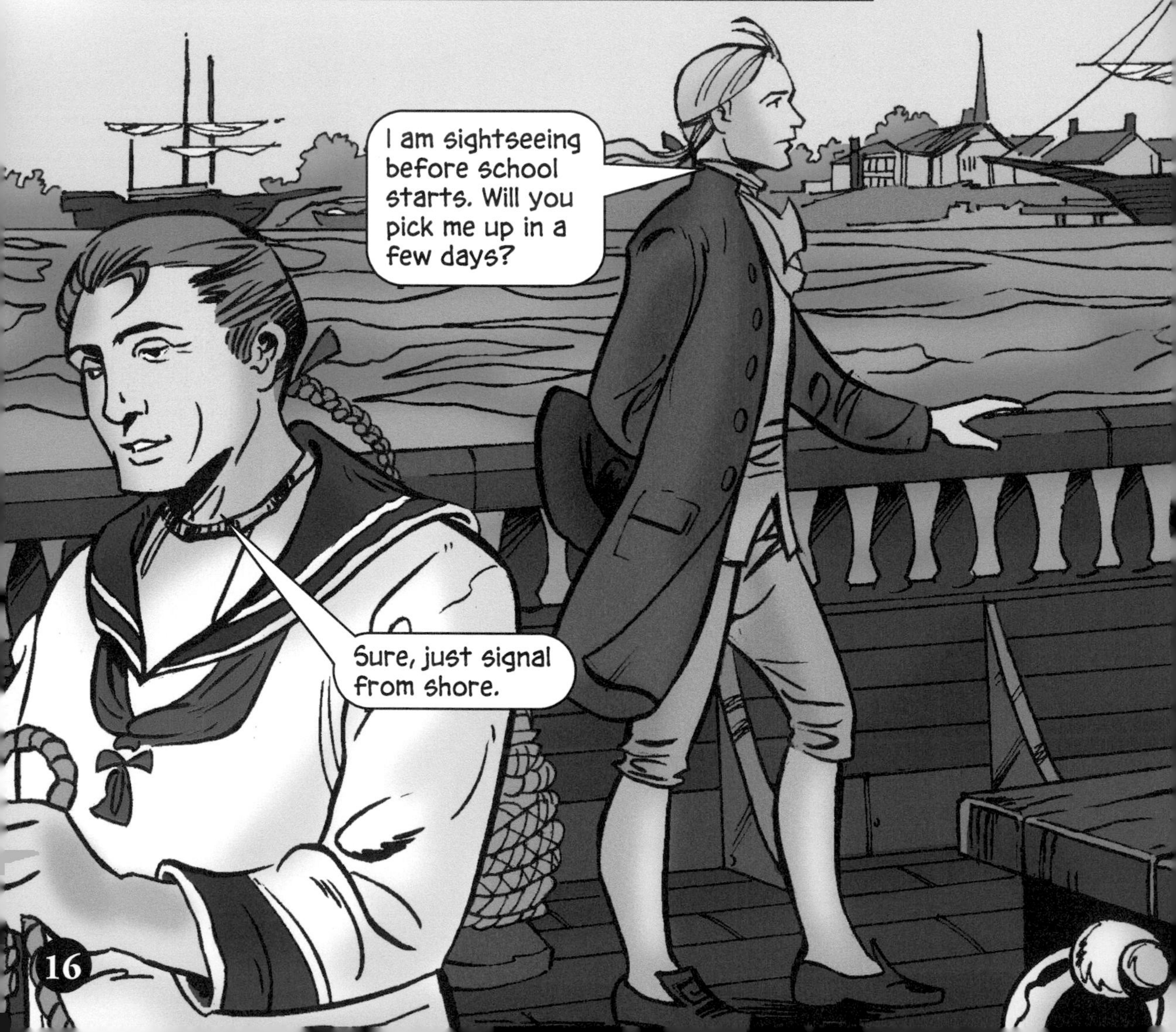

I am sightseeing before school starts. Will you pick me up in a few days?
Sure, just signal from shore.

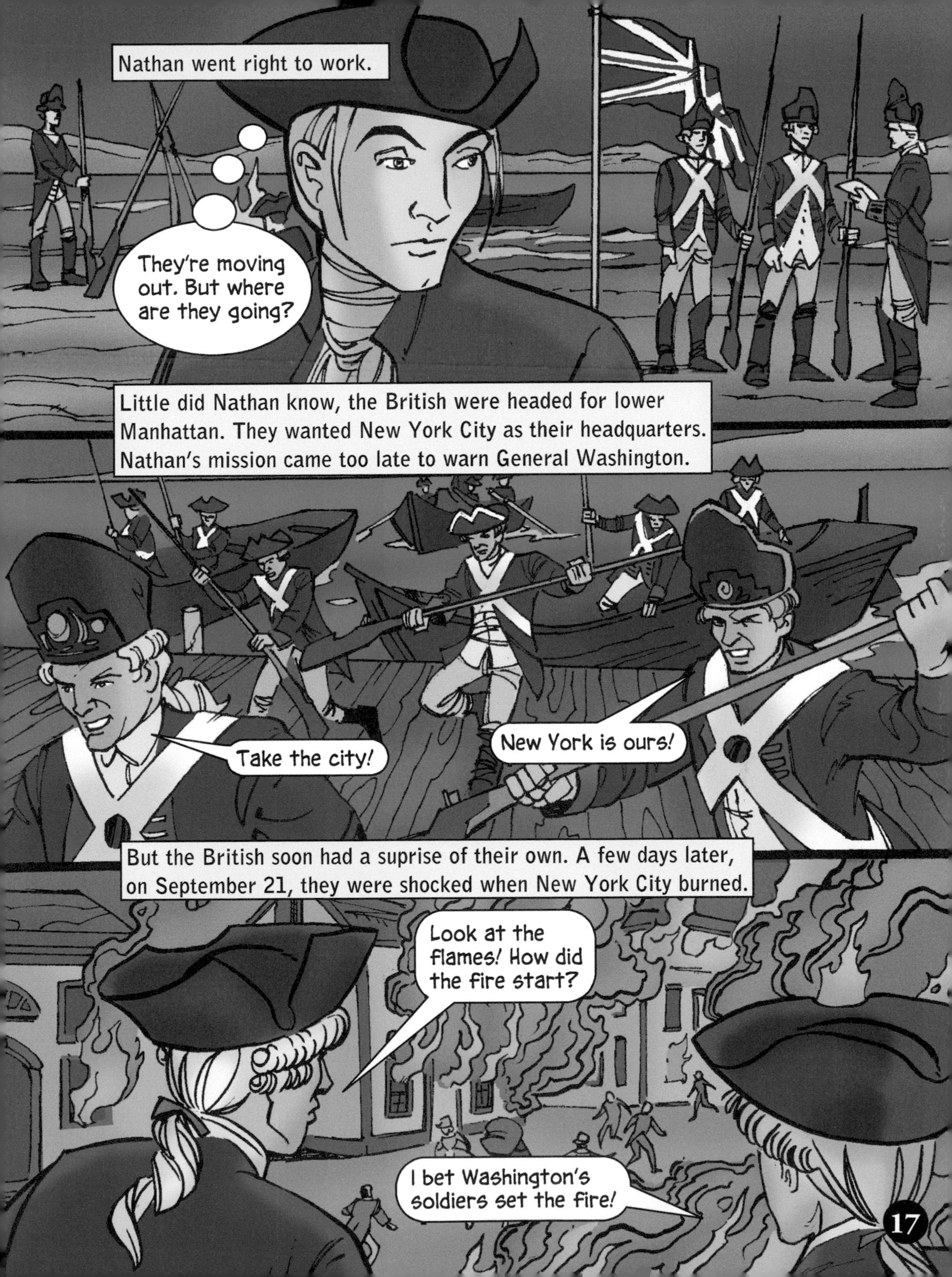
Nathan went right to work.
They're moving out. But where are they going?
Little did Nathan know, the British were headed for lower Manhattan. They wanted New York City as their headquarters. Nathan's mission came too late to warn General Washington.
Take the city!
New York is ours!
But the British soon had a suprise of their own. A few days later, on September 21, they were shocked when New York City burned.
Look at the flames! How did the fire start?
I bet Washington's soldiers set the fire!

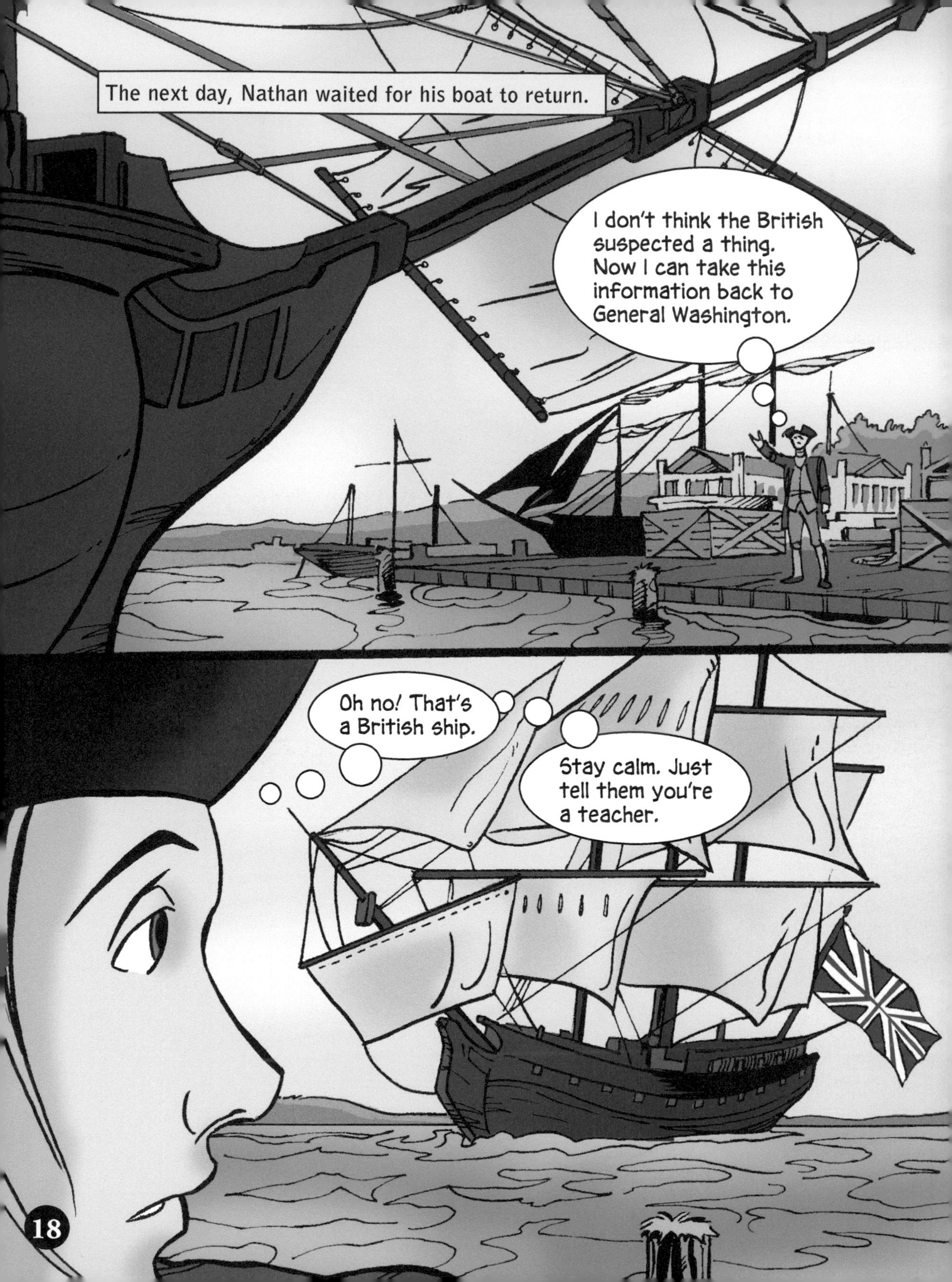
The next day, Nathan waited for his boat to return.
I don't think the British suspected a thing. Now I can take this information back to General Washington.
Oh no! That's a British ship.
Stay calm. Just tell them you're a teacher.

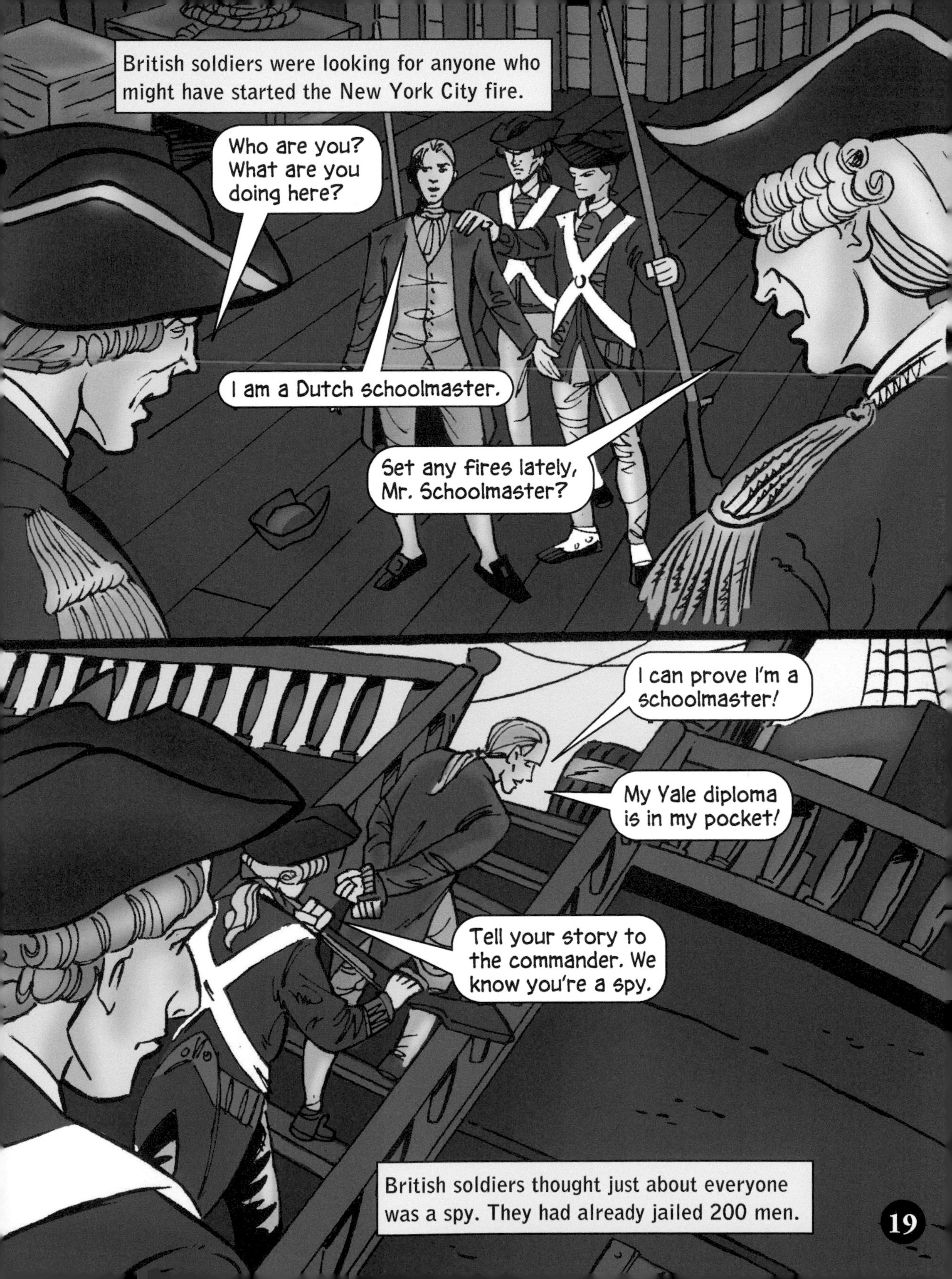
British soldiers were looking for anyone who might have started the New York City fire.
Who are you? What are you doing here?
I am a Dutch schoolmaster.
Set any fires lately, Mr. Schoolmaster?
I can prove I'm a schoolmaster!
My Yale diploma is in my pocket!
Tell your story to the commander. We know you're a spy.
British soldiers thought just about everyone was a spy. They had already jailed 200 men.

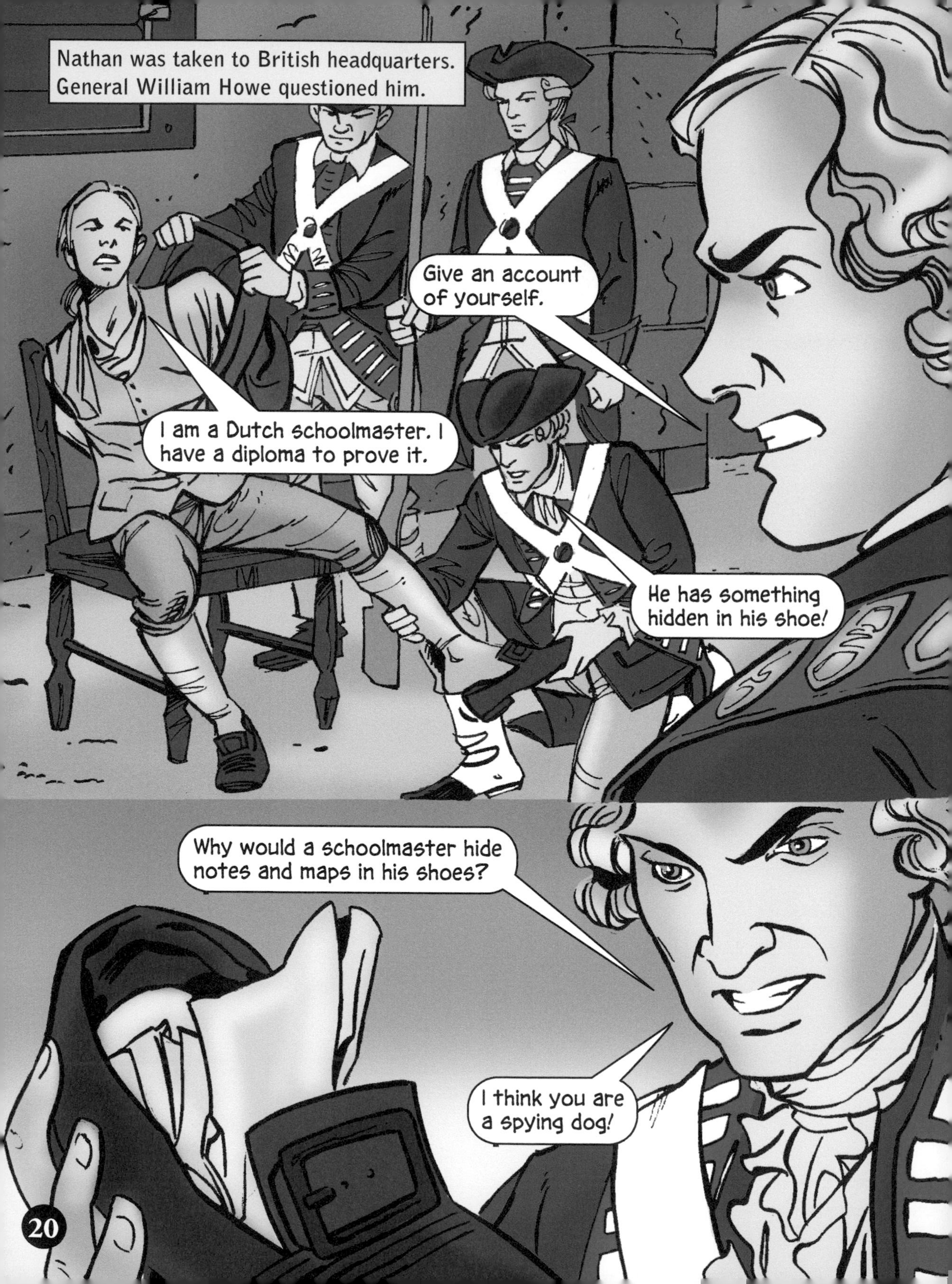
Nathan was taken to British headquarters. General William Howe questioned him.
Give an account of yourself.
I am a Dutch schoolmaster. I have a diploma to prove it.
He has something hidden in his shoe!
Why would a schoolmaster hide notes and maps in his shoes?
I think you are a spying dog!

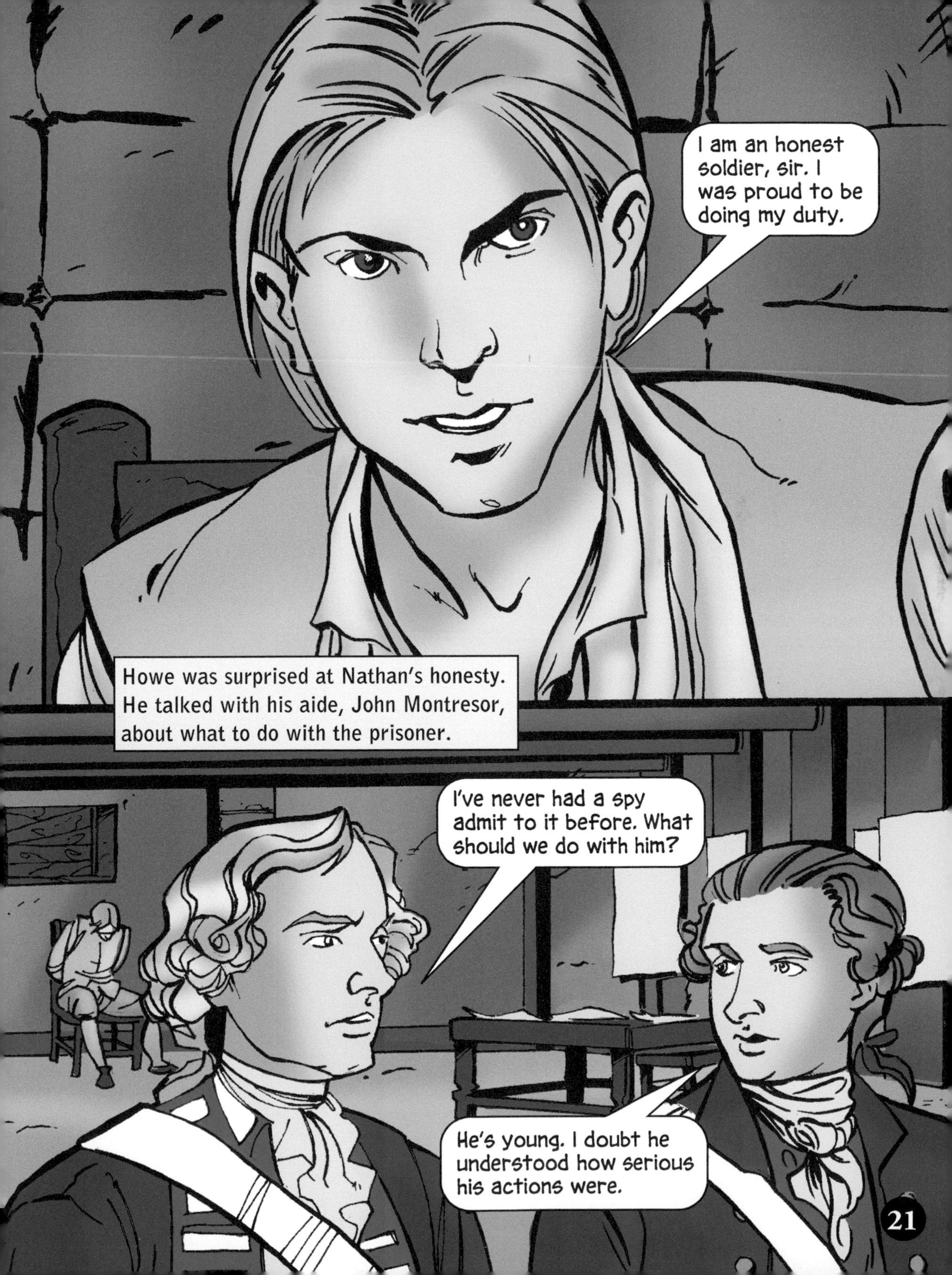
I am an honest soldier, sir. I was proud to be doing my duty.
Howe was surprised at Nathan's honesty. He talked with his aide, John Montresor, about what to do with the prisoner.
I've never had a spy admit to it before. What should we do with him?
He's young. I doubt he understood how serious his actions were.

CHAPTER 4

WAR HERO

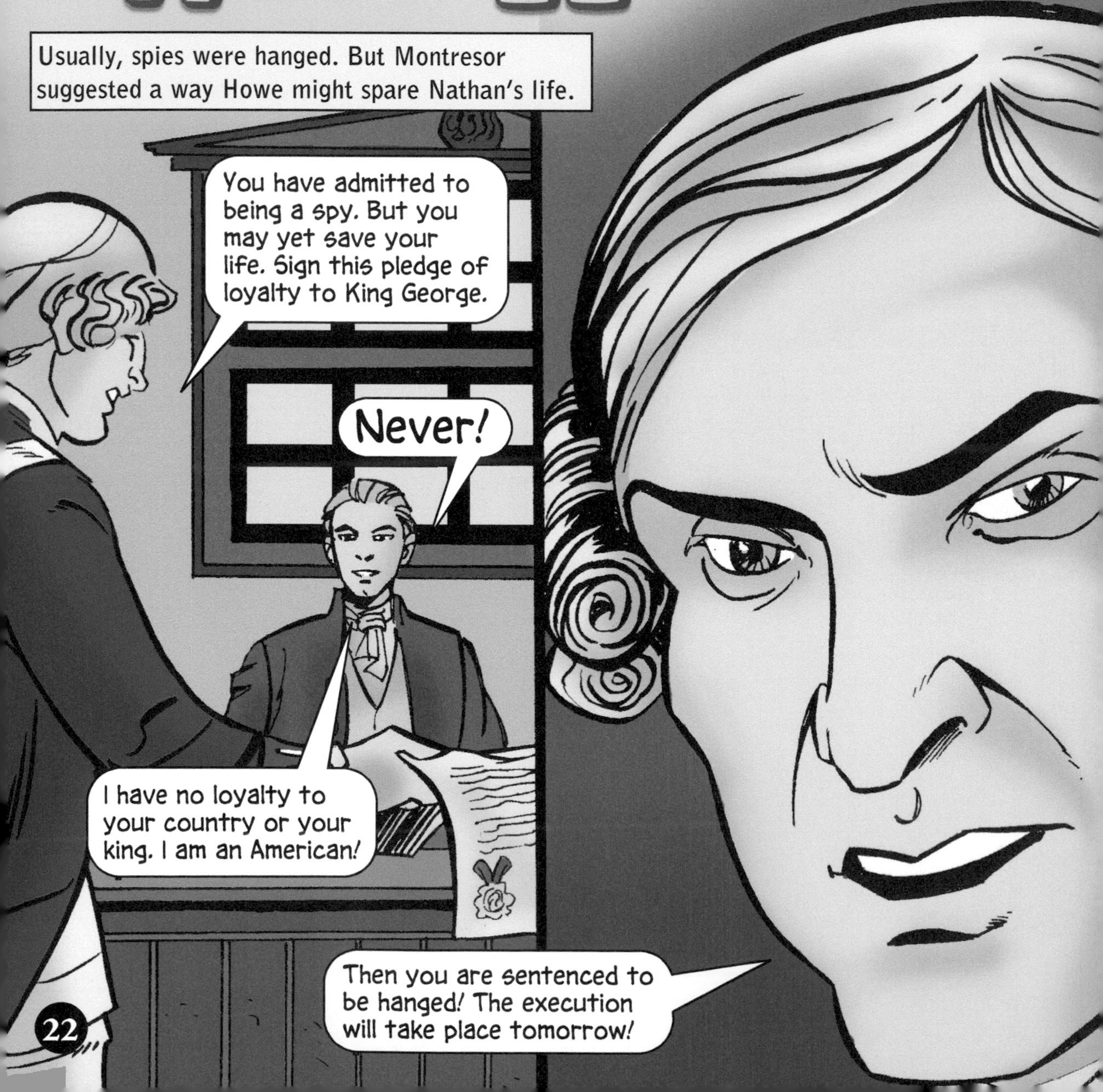

Usually, spies were hanged. But Montresor suggested a way Howe might spare Nathan's life.
You have admitted to being a spy. But you may yet save your life. Sign this pledge of loyalty to King George.
Never!
I have no loyalty to your country or your king. I am an American!
Then you are sentenced to be hanged! The execution will take place tomorrow!

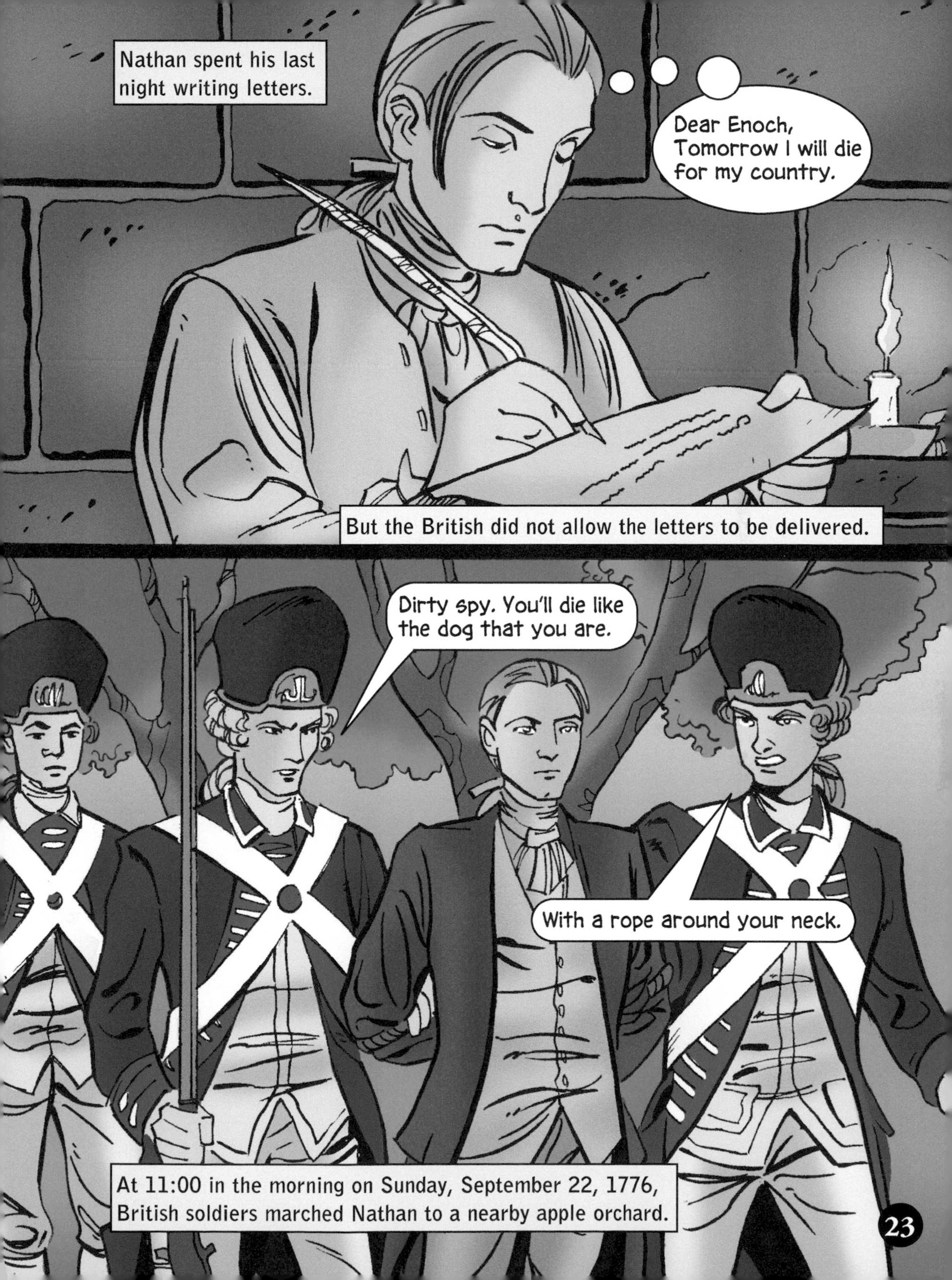
Nathan spent his last night writing letters.
Dear Enoch, Tomorrow I will die for my country.
But the British did not allow the letters to be delivered.
Dirty spy. You'll die like the dog that you are.
With a rope around your neck.
At 11:00 in the morning on Sunday, September 22, 1776, British soldiers marched Nathan to a nearby apple orchard.

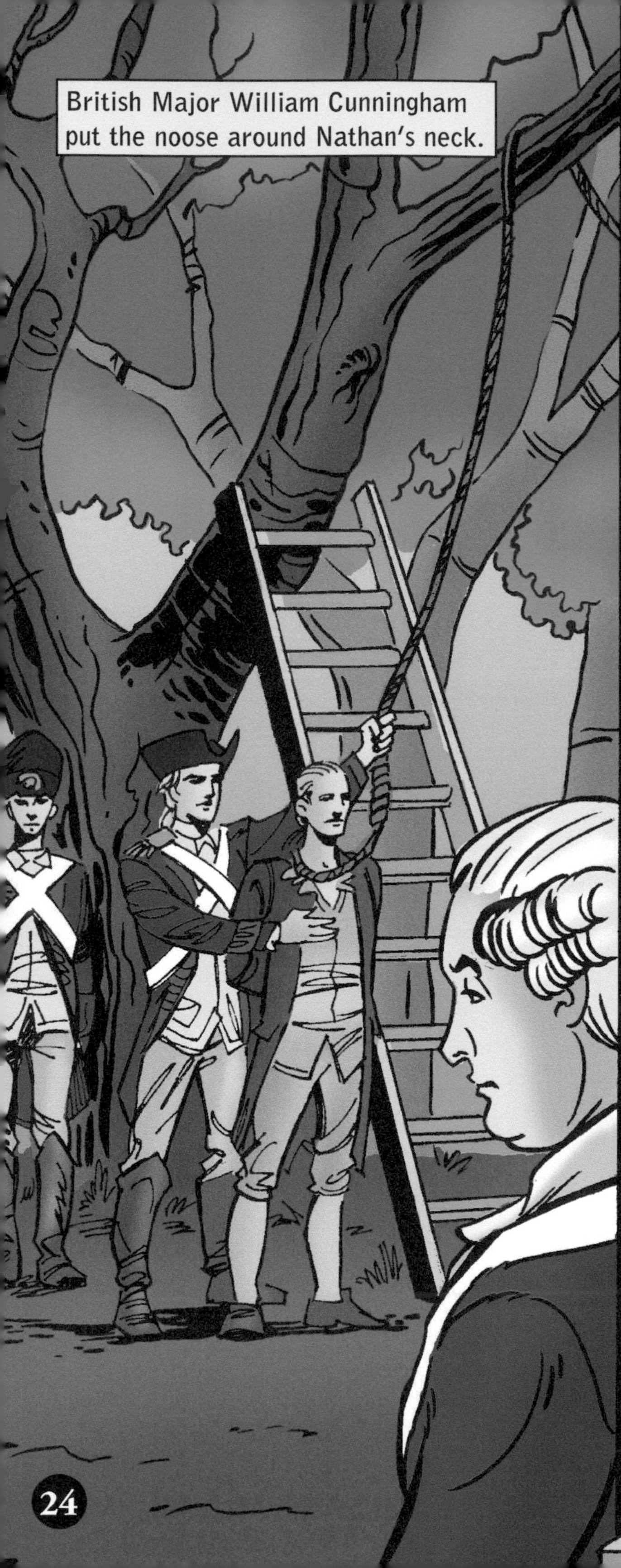
British Major William Cunningham put the noose around Nathan's neck.

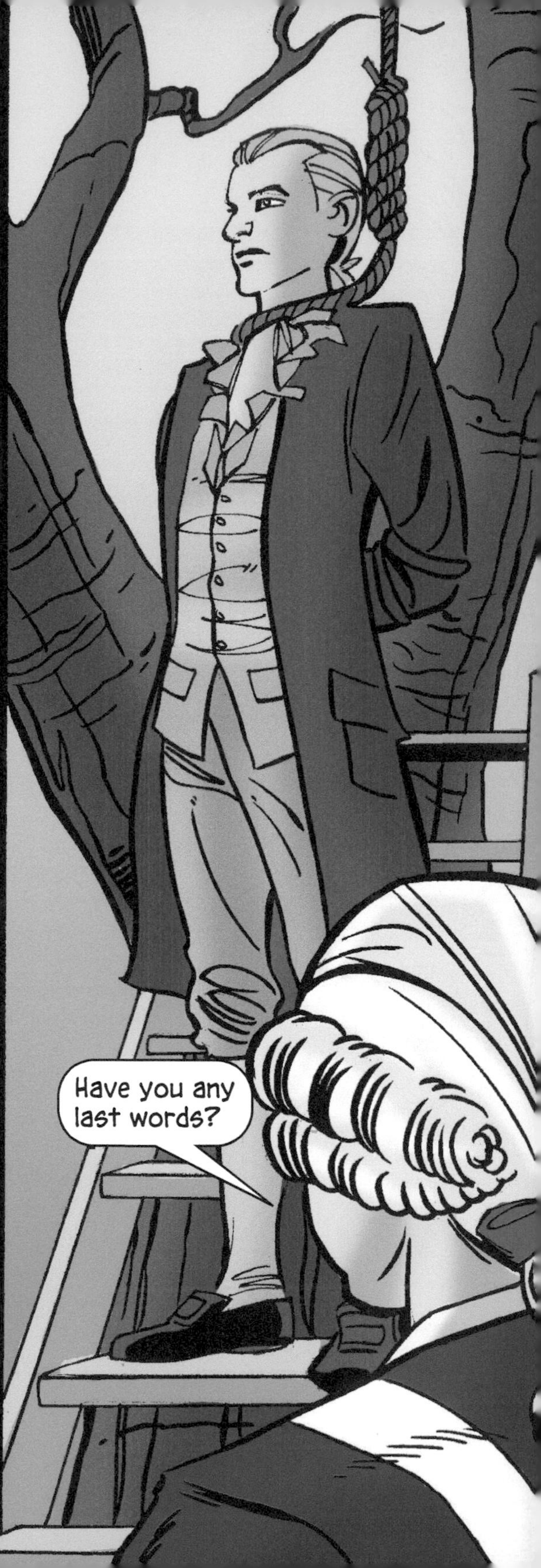
Have you any last words?

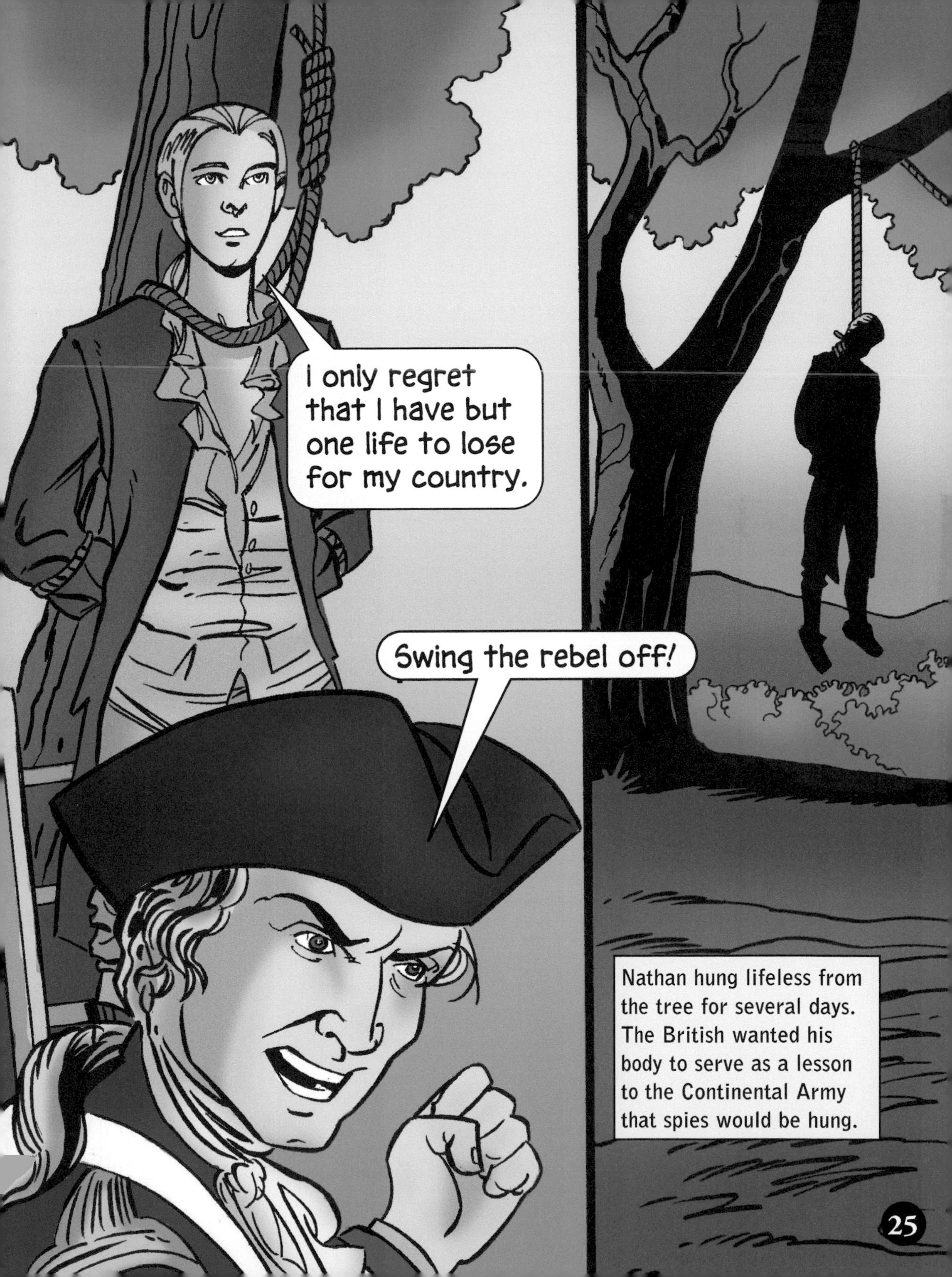
I only regret that I have but one life to lose for my country.
Swing the rebel off!
Nathan hung lifeless from the tree for several days. The British wanted his body to serve as a lesson to the Continental Army that spies would be hung.

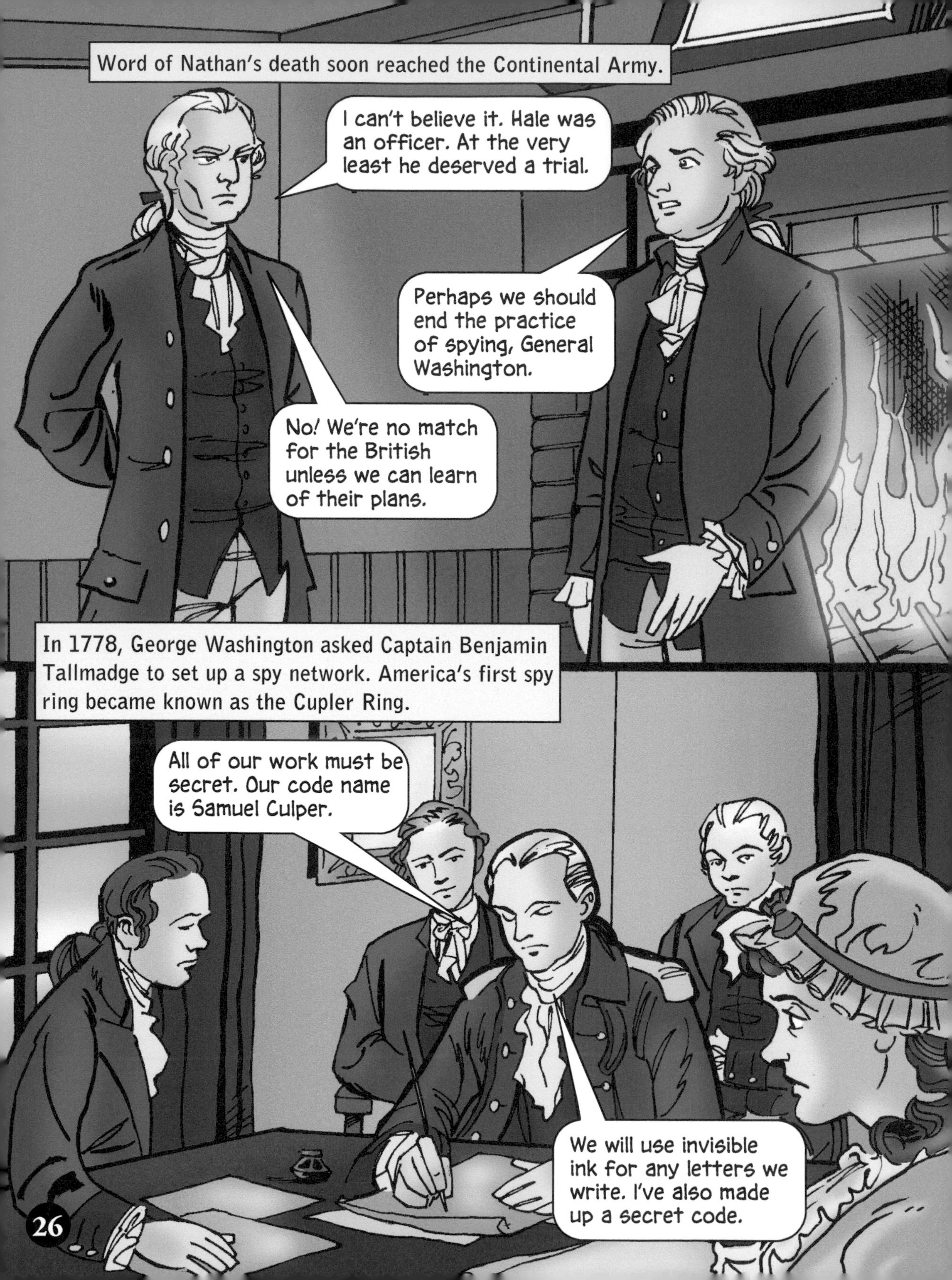
Word of Nathan's death soon reached the Continental Army.
I can't believe it. Hale was an officer. At the very least he deserved a trial.
Perhaps we should end the practice of spying, General Washington.
No! We're no match for the British unless we can learn of their plans.
In 1778, George Washington asked Captain Benjamin Tallmadge to set up a spy network. America's first spy ring became known as the Cupler Ring.
All of our work must be secret. Our code name is Samuel Culper.
We will use invisible ink for any letters we write. I've also made up a secret code.

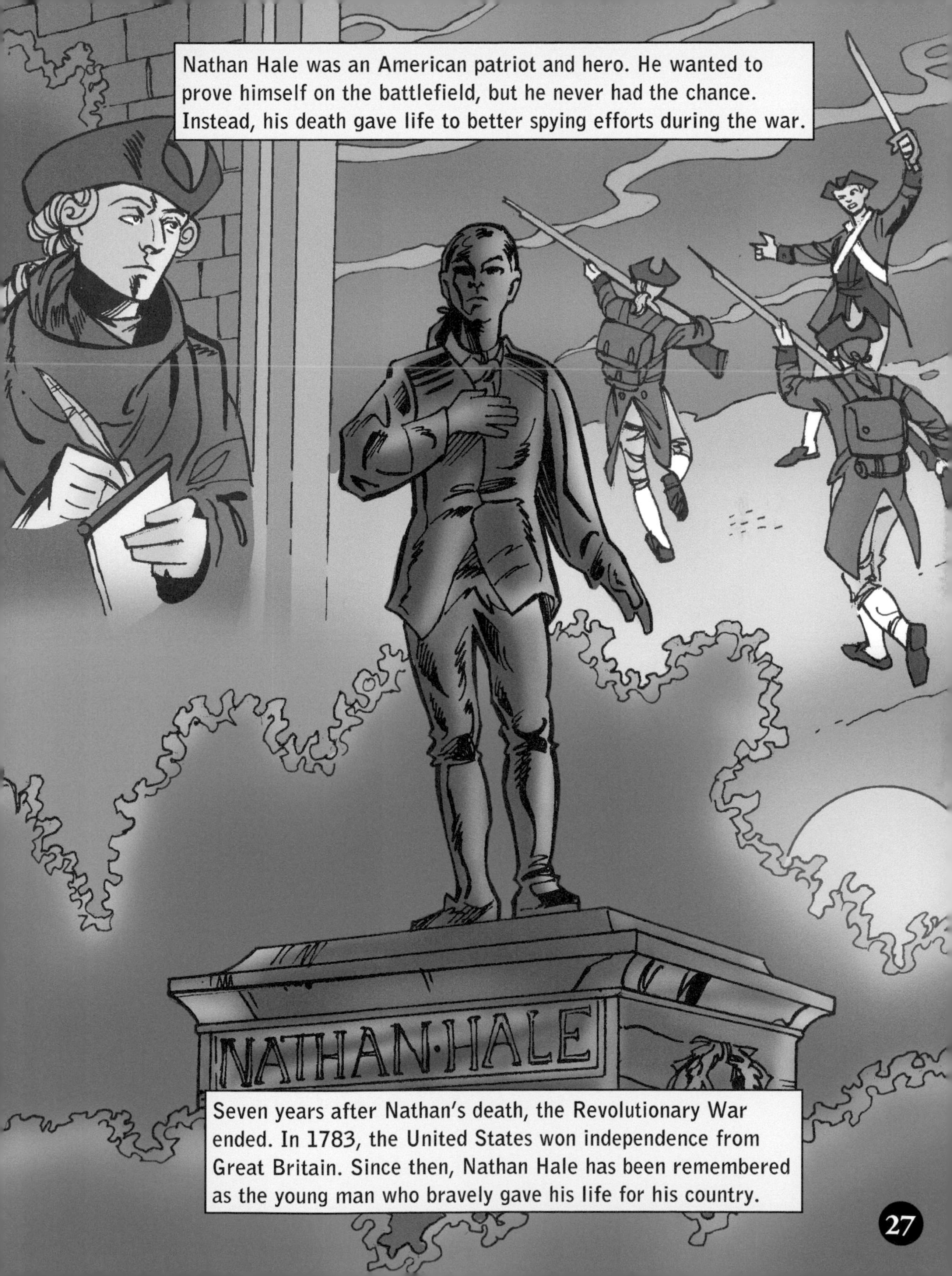
Nathan Hale was an American patriot and hero. He wanted to prove himself on the battlefield, but he never had the chance. Instead, his death gave life to better spying efforts during the war.
NATHAN·HALE
Seven years after Nathan's death, the Revolutionary War ended. In 1783, the United States won independence from Great Britain. Since then, Nathan Hale has been remembered as the young man who bravely gave his life for his country.

MORE ABOUT

NATHAN HALE

- Nathan Hale was born June 6, 1755, in Coventry, Connecticut. He died September 22, 1776. He was 21.

- Five of Nathan's seven brothers served in the military. Only Nathan died during the Revolutionary War.

- Enoch Hale and Nathan exchanged many letters while Nathan was in the army. In 1784, Enoch's first son was born. He was named Nathan Hale.

- Nathan's nephew once said of his famous uncle, "He was a simple-hearted, well-educated, intelligent country youth, always doing what he thought right. He died conscious that he had done right, and only regretting that the sudden end to which he was brought, rendered it impossible for him to do more good."

- A silhouette was traced on a door of Nathan's childhood home. Many people believe the outline is of Nathan. Portraits and statues of Nathan have been based on this silhouette.

🦅 Nathan's body was buried in an unmarked grave, probably in New York. After his death, Nathan's family built a memorial, called a cenotaph, in Coventry cemetery. The inscription reads, "He resigned his life—a sacrifice to his country's liberty at New York, September 1776."

🦅 William Hull was Nathan's good friend. Hull went to John Montresor and asked him for details of Nathan's death. Montresor felt badly about what had happened. "He might have been better treated," Montresor told Hull. "War brings out the worst in people. And, I suppose, the best. [Nathan] was an extraordinary young man. I will never forget him."

🦅 Nathan kept a diary. It spans the time he left New London, Connecticut, until his military company entered New York. Some pages are torn from the diary. What remains begins September 23, 1775, and ends on August 23, 1776.

🦅 In 1985, Nathan became Connecticut's official state hero.

GLOSSARY

debate (di-BAYT)—a discussion that considers the arguments for or against something

diploma (duh-PLOH-muh)—a certificate from a school showing a person finished a course of study

network (NET-wurk)—a group of people who share information with each other

regiment (REJ-uh-muhnt)—a military unit consisting of about 1,000 soldiers

sloop (SLOOP)—a sailboat with one mast and sails that are set from front to back

INTERNET SITES

FactHound offers a safe, fun way to find Internet sites related to this book. All of the sites on FactHound have been researched by our staff.

Here's how:

1. *Visit www.facthound.com*
2. Type in this special code **0736849688** for age-appropriate sites. Or enter a search word related to this book for a more general search.
3. Click on the **Fetch It** button.

FactHound will fetch the best sites for you!

READ MORE

Cefrey, Holly. *"One Life to Lose for My Country": The Arrest and Execution of Nathan Hale*. Great Moments in American History. New York: Rosen, 2004

Devillier, Christy. *Nathan Hale*. First Biographies. Edina, Minn.: Abdo, 2004.

Kneib, Martha. *Women Soldiers, Spies, and Patriots of the American Revolution*. American Women at War. New York: Rosen, 2004.

Marquette, Scott. *Revolutionary War*. America at War. Vero Beach, Fla.: Rourke, 2003.

BIBLIOGRAPHY

Johnston, Henry Phelps. *Nathan Hale 1776: Biography and Memorials*. New Haven, Conn.: Yale University Press, 1914.

Seymour, George Dudley. *Documentary Life of Nathan Hale: Comprising All Available Official and Private Documents Bearing on the Life of the Patriot*. New Haven, Conn.: Private Publisher, 1941.

Stuart, I. W. *Life of Captain Nathan Hale: The Martyr-Spy of the American Revolution*. Hartford, Conn.: F.A. Brown, 1856.

INDEX

7th Connecticut Regiment,
10
19th Continental Regiment,
11, 12

Boston Massacre, 7
Boston Tea Party, 9
British taxes, 4–5, 9

Cunningham, William, 24,
25
Cupler Ring, 26

education of girls, 7, 8

Hale, Enoch (brother), 4, 5,
23, 28
Hale, Nathan
   birth of, 28
   bravery of, 13, 14, 15,
      21, 22, 24–25, 27
   capture of, 19–21
   childhood of, 4–5
   death of, 25, 26, 27, 28,
      29
   diary of, 11, 29
   education of, 5, 6–7
   as soldier, 10–11, 12–13,
      14
   as spy, 15, 16–18

   as teacher, 8
Hale, Richard (father), 4, 5
Howe, William, 20–21, 22
Hull, William, 15, 29

Knowlton's Rangers, 14, 15
Knowlton, Thomas, 14, 15

Montresor, John, 21, 22, 29

New York City, 12, 14, 17,
   19, 29

Revolutionary War
   end of, 27
   start of, 10

Stamp Act, 4

Tallmadge, Benjamin, 26

Union School, 8

Washington, George, 12, 14,
   15, 17, 18, 26
Webb, Charles, 10

Yale College, 5, 6–7